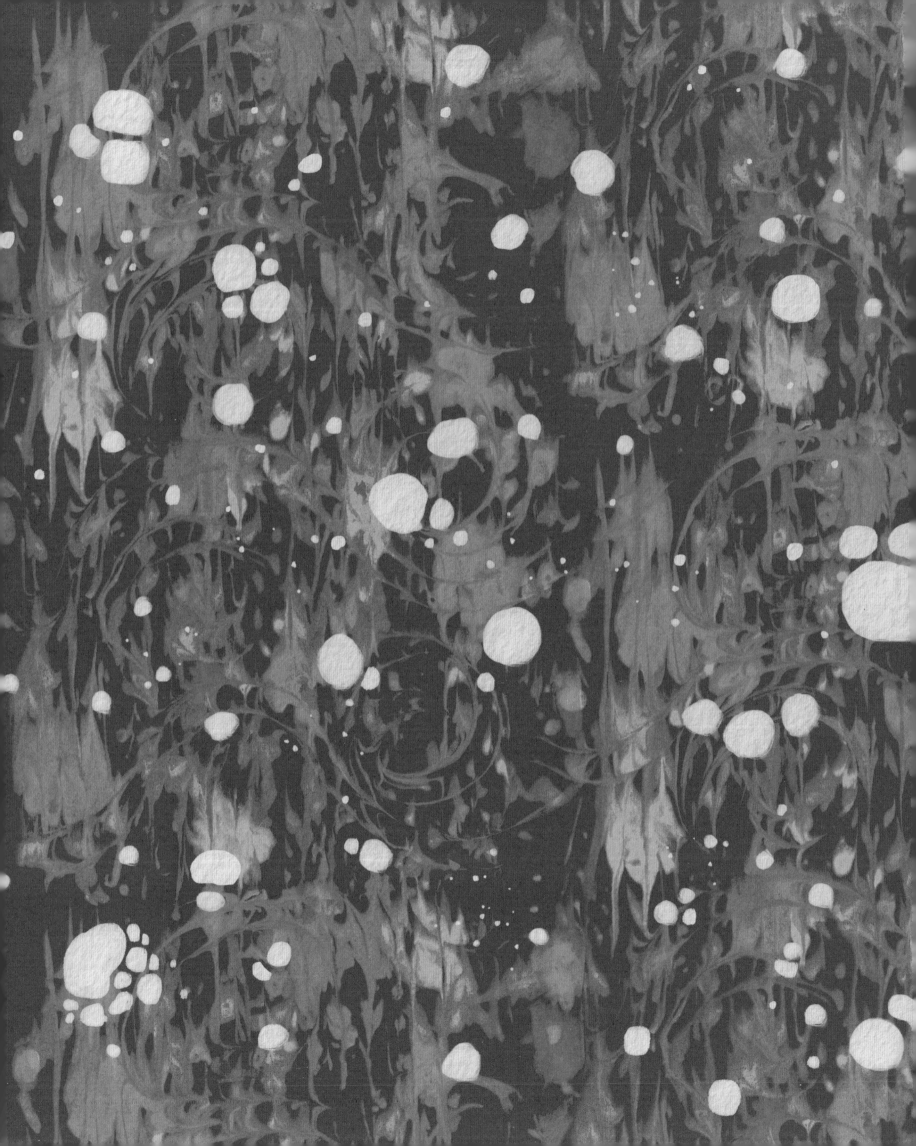

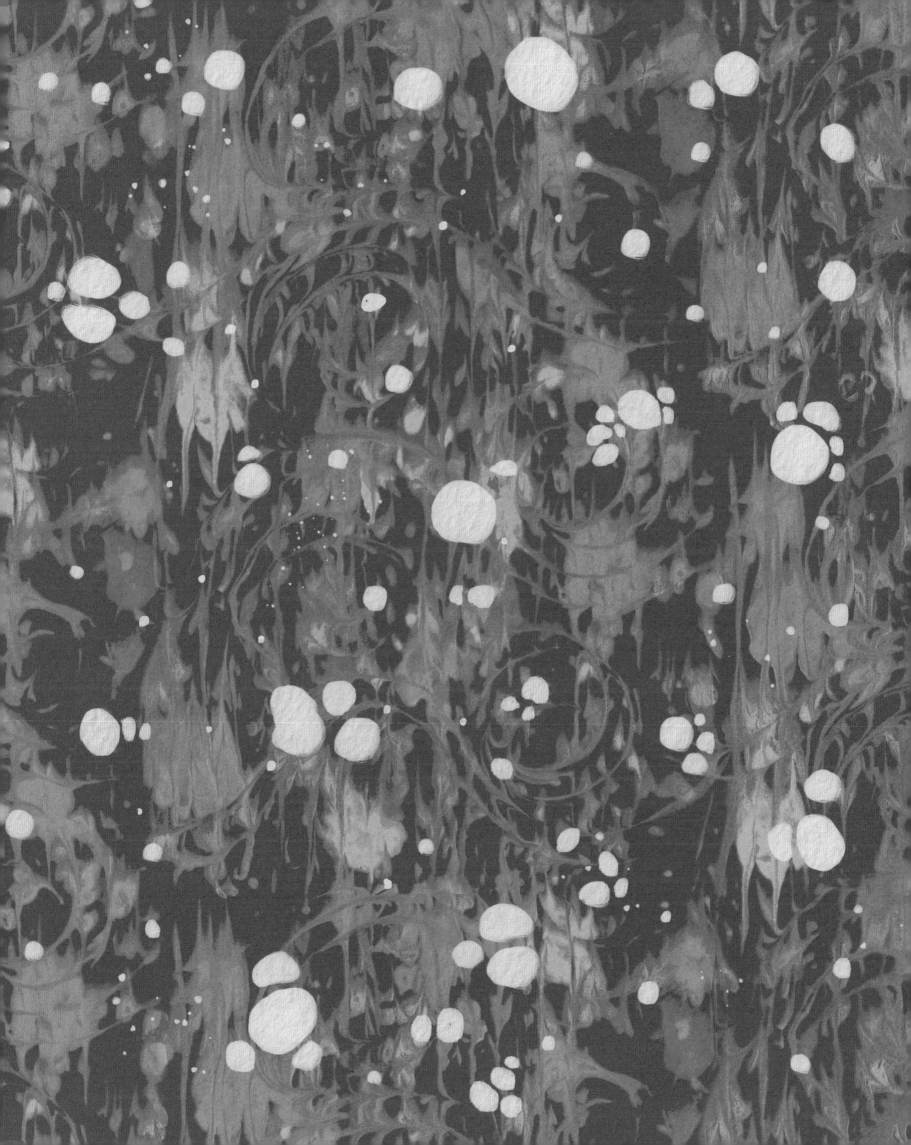

For Matteo—to many more turns around the Sun—L.B.

For my mum, who has always nurtured my curiosity about the natural world—M.S.A.

Brimming with creative inspiration, how-to projects, and useful information to enrich your everyday life, The Quarto Group is a favorite destination for those pursuing their interests and passions. Visit our site and dig deeper with our books into your area of interest: Quarto Creates, Quarto Cooks, Quarto Homes, Quarto Lives, Quarto Drives, Quarto Explores, Quarto Gifts, or Quarto Kids.

First Published in 2022 by Wide Eyed Editions,
an imprint of The Quarto Group.
100 Cummings Center, Suite 265D, Beverly, MA 01915 USA.
T +1 978-282-9590 F +1 978-283-2742 www.Quarto.com

ISBN 978-0-7112-6966-8
eISBN 978-0-7112-6967-5

The illustrations were created digitally
Set in Meltow, Cream, Brandon Grotesque and Futura

Published by Georgia Amson-Bradshaw
Commissioned by Lucy Brownridge
Designed by Karissa Santos
Copy-edited by Rose Blackett-Ord
Production by Dawn Cameron

Manufactured in Guangdong, China CC022022

9 8 7 6 5 4 3 2 1

What are you doing today, Mother Nature?

written by Lucy Brownridge

illustrated by Margaux Samson Abadie

WIDE EYED EDITIONS

STORIES

In the high Japanese mountains, snow is heavy and winds are bitterly cold. A family of monkeys is chilled to the bone as they traverse carefully down a slope into Jigokudani Park.

Amid the crunchy ice is a pool of steaming water, naturally bubbling up from the depths of the Earth's core.

A baby monkey plops into the pool, followed by a grandma monkey. Grandma cups the warm water in her hands and brings it up to her face to wash away the ice crystals on her brow.

The baby nestles into her warm fur, and she puts her arm around him. He has done so well, out on the mountain all day!

The whole family closes their eyes, and their bodies relax as nature's hot bath washes away the cold of a long, treacherous day.

JAPAN
A Hot Bath in Winter

Of all the monkeys, Japanese macaques live furthest north, and in January life is very chilly indeed for them. Monkeys are not so different from us, and after a long day on the icy mountaintops, there is only one way they like to warm up.

PERU
The Great Parrot Clay Lick

The brightest and flashiest residents of the forest are the macaws, and showtime is about to begin. January is time to dust off their tail feathers and prepare for mating season. The first item on the agenda is breakfast! But looking your best can come at a price, and sometimes it means a strange diet.

Deep in the Amazon rainforest, huge clay banks line the river's edge. The brownish-red earth looks dull compared to the vibrant forest, but as the Sun comes up it will soon be transformed into a fluttering technicolor breakfast buffet.

In January, the walls of the riverbanks teem with macaws from all around the forest. They fill their beaks with clay, and then take it back to their nests to eat.

This clay is filled with important minerals, which every macaw worth its salt needs in order to look and feel its very best.

The macaws come back every morning in a rainbow formation to dine on the muddiest of breakfasts. Each time they visit, they get more of the essential nutrients that are lacking in the rest of their diet.

When they are at the peak of their health and fully topped up on their clay cleanse, they are ready to find a mate and start a family.

ANTARCTICA
A Little Chick's Very Long Day

In the Antarctic, January is midsummer—and a time when little Adélie penguin chicks have only just hatched. They pop out onto the ice, surrounded by other families and by their fluffy, loving parents. But their first day is the longest on Earth!

This little chick is just a few moments old. She stares up at her parents and into the bright shining Sun above. She lives in the Antarctic, where the South Pole of the Earth is.

She learns to waddle...

and slide...

and eat delicious fish from mum's beak

14

It's been a busy day for this little chick—but when bedtime comes, the Sun doesn't set! Instead, she huddles inside mum's fluffy down and shuts her eyes to sleep.

At this time of year, the Antarctic is facing towards the Sun for 24 hours a day. The Sun stays in the sky day and night during the Antarctic summer, and so night doesn't truly come until winter.

As a chick, this little one will only ever know endless sunshine and summer.

AFGHANISTAN
Love in a Snowstorm

January spells snowstorm season in the rocky Wakhan Corridor. It is the highest part of Afghanistan, and home to a powerful lone ranger. This snow leopard is prowling her huge territory as the first storm of the season blows in.

She is a magnificent creature, and she is not scared of anything—she can chase down her prey over the most challenging landscapes. She lives life alone, and in charge.

But as winter nears its coldest and darkest point, she starts to call out into the blizzard for the first time. She leaves messages by rubbing her smell onto trees and rocks.

She wanders for days and finally, when she is at the top of a perilous cliff, she hears a reply.

She bounds through the falling snow, across cascading rocks, to meet the male snow leopard she's been calling for. He followed her scent trail. It is a miracle that over such huge distances they have found each other.

The pair mate, and a few months later, the love of her life arrives in the form of a little cub. For a few special months, the snow leopard will know what it is like not to live alone.

One day her cub will leave her side to lead a life alone, just like her mother—until the moment comes when she, too, makes her call into the wild, in search of love.

February

JAPAN
A Blush of Pink

From winter cold bursts a sudden bloom of cherry-pink blossoms, and soon southern Japan blushes with the promise of spring.

This tree has stood bare all winter long. But over the last month, the jagged branches have felt little buds of green springing up along their lengths.

Now each bud swells. Things are growing inside, until…

First one bud pops, then another. Once green and shut, now they open into bright pink blooms, the rosy tint giving hope for warmer days to come.

This is not just the story of one flower or one tree, but of a million, all blooming in a great wave that sweeps Japan. Nature wakes up after the long night of winter, and gives the world a message written in flowers:

"It is morning!"

In Japanese, cherry blossom is called "sakura."

MEXICO
A Kaleidoscope of Butterflies

It is February in Mexico, and an amazing finale is about to take place. But to understand our story, we must wind back the clock to the end of summer in Canada. A monarch butterfly hatches from his chrysalis. Emerging at this time of year means that he is destined for a big quest. Normally a monarch lives for four weeks, but those born in late summer will live for up to nine months. He has a big destiny to fulfil, and a long trip ahead.

Canadian winters are too cold for monarch butterflies, so he takes an extra-long sip of nectar and sets off on a 2,500-mile journey.

For two months, the little butterfly flies throughout each day, all the way south across North America.

Like his ancestors before him, he is leaving Canada for the warm volcanic mountains of central Mexico. He doesn't need directions; his body knows where to take him.

Finally, tired out, the butterfly lands softly on a remote mountaintop. At first it seems he is alone, and the trunks and branches appear to be blanketed with rusty fall leaves. Is this the right spot? Is the journey over?

A closer look reveals that they aren't leaves at all. They are quivering! As the Sun emerges from behind a cloud to warm them, hundreds of thousands of monarch butterflies take to the sky. They make the whole hillside hum with the beating of their wings.

This must be the place his body was telling him to come to! The butterflies cluster together on the trees, sip the cool, clear dew, and prepare to lay millions of eggs.

Come spring, their eggs will hatch, and in time new generations will follow in the delicate wingbeats of their adventurous ancestors.

WALES
A Cloud of Frog Spawn

Deep in the rainwashed valleys of Wales, ancient glades and shaded dells are still and cold. But in the pools of water left by hard February rain, something miraculous is about to happen.

It's wonderful weather for frogs, and the pools are filled with them. When they mate, the female frog releases lots of little wibbly blobs, each with a tiny black pinprick at its center.

The cloud of wobbling jellies sits just below the water like a tiny universe. Each black pinprick is a future frog. A bird comes by and gulps down a few little jellies, but there are plenty left.

"Some for the rook, some for the crow, some will perish—but lots will grow."

0–4 weeks: A baby tadpole hatches. It has a long tail and visible gills. At 10 days old, it starts grazing on algae.

6–7 weeks: Speckles appear, and the tadpole eats larger pieces of food.

Day by day, the little blobs begin to wriggle… and then turn into longer blobs with tails. With added tail power, they wriggle SO hard that they burst out from their wibbly jellies and into the pool.

7–14 weeks: Legs sprout, starting at the back. First 'knees' grow, and then whole, double-jointed limbs. Lungs also develop.

14–16 weeks: All four legs are complete, and the tail has gone.

Week by week they grow, sprouting new, strong sets of legs. Tail power is replaced by leg power, until their tails disappear altogether. What was once a universe of tiny black stars is now a hopping, jumping forest floor full of tiny frogs.

USA
A Super Bloom in Death Valley

This hot, craggy landscape in California is a place of extremes. Its frightening name is a warning that life hangs in the balance here. You won't spot many plants on this rocky landscape, but that doesn't mean that seeds aren't lying in wait below the ground. Every few years, if the weather is just right, an almighty show takes place on this otherwise dusty stage.

CAUTION! EXTREME HEAT DANGER

There is no rain for much of the year. The heat beats down on the rocks, day after hot Californian day.

But this winter, now and again, there have been showers of rain. The start of the year has been very still, and no wind has come to wick away the precious water from the thirsty earth.

Water seeps through the parched soil and soaks a little seed. For miles around, seeds have their first drink, and suddenly millions of tiny lives are electrified.

The plants begin to unfurl and grow from their hard-shelled seeds, pushing out into the warming air.

By the middle of February, the brown desert landscape has been transformed. The kaleidoscope of color, abuzz with bugs flitting from bloom to bloom, is a reminder from the valley. Even in a landscape of danger and extremes, nature's unstoppable life force is never far away!

Desert Trumpet

Death Valley Monkey Flower

Grape Soda Lupine

Desert Gold

Sand Verbena

Mariposa Lily

Desert Paintbrush

March

NETHERLANDS
Life Springs from the Rich Earth

Every March, spring bulbs bloom from the Dutch earth in their millions and spread across the country like a wild tulip frenzy. This colorful, canal-checked landscape is a story of Mother Nature and people working together.

Ever since the 1600s, this place has been the home of spring bulbs. Merchants brought bulbs from all around the world and grew them here.

The weather and the rich earth in this low-lying land are just right for blooming extra-big flowers.

Tulip bulbs became so precious here that a long time ago they were even used instead of money.

This country still grows more tulips and other bulbs than any other country on Earth, and it is home to the best spring displays of flowers.

CANADA
A Frog Defrosts

Canadian winters are cold and long, and many animals have had to adapt to living in the deep freeze by growing dense fur, or hibernating in warm dens until spring. But one particular frog doesn't even try to stay warm.

In March, the ground is starting to thaw, but many lakes and ponds are still frozen. Beneath some crisp leaf mulch by a lake, a little frog is hidden, frozen solid. He isn't breathing and he has no pulse. He looks as though he must have been killed in the harsh winter.

But just as the lakes change state and return to life, so does this little frog. His body produces natural antifreeze, which means that he can thaw out and come back to life undamaged.

From the inside out, he thaws, and his heart starts beating. His brain awakens; he blinks a chilly eyelid over a frost-clouded eye. Eventually he moves around, recharged by the warming sun.

This miraculous frog hops into spring, perfectly healthy and defrosted, rejuvenated by the life-giving warmth of the sun.

DENMARK
A Black Sun Ballet

In the grassy marshlands of Jutland in Denmark, an eclipse like no other is about to take place.
Other eclipses you might read about happen when a planet or moon blocks the Sun's rays.
But the black Sun, or "sort sol" in Danish, is just a little different.

The Sun is setting, and the starlings who live in the Tønder marshlands are beginning their evening routine.

At this time of year, there are many more of them than usual. Thousands have stopped here on their migration between their wintering grounds further south in Europe and their Baltic summer retreats.

As the Sun dips below the horizon and spectacular sunset colors flood the skies, the birds take to the wing. There are up to one million birds all at once, and from a distance they are like a shimmering ball of blackness in the sky. Moving as one, the murmuration of birds is so thick in the sky that the sunset is turned almost entirely black.

The flock ripples and twists, performing a kind of sky ballet as, for a moment, their power and beauty triumph over the Sun.

When all is done, the Sun and the birds leave the sky still and dark, suddenly empty. There is a dramatic pause—until tomorrow evening's performance.

MEXICO
Gray Whales

It is March in Mexico, and the lagoons of Baja California are sparkling in the warm air. But this month, if you look closely at the crest of a wave, you might spot the dorsal ridge of a gentle giant who has traveled many miles to be here for a very special event.

A gray whale has arrived in the lagoon after a long swim—all the way here from the chilly Arctic. She goes to the Arctic each year for the food, but in March she always returns, with a full tummy, for the Mexican weather.

At this time of year, the gray whales' social scene is thriving along this beautiful coast, and it is the perfect place to find love.

March is the time when many animals find a partner and start a family, and this whale is no different.

A few months later, her calf is born and all along the lagoon little whales are taking their first swims. They are building up their strength to swim all the way back to the Arctic to feast on fish come the winter.

April

NEPAL
A Cascade of Snow

High in the Himalayan mountains, snow has been falling for months—all through the winter.

As a single flake lands, it looks weightless and magical. But in fact, when packed layer upon layer, these lacy flurries of frozen water become heavy. As the weight builds, it is harder for the snowpack to stay in place.

Small animals run across the packed snow, but it stays put.

A big gust of wind comes along and blows a tiny top layer off the powder, but the rest keeps its grip on the side of the slope.

But one day, a sudden spring snowfall descends on the steep slope. As snow builds up higher and higher, the weight is too much!

The whole area of snow cascades down, tumbling in an icy cloud right to the very bottom.

ENGLAND
A Blanket of Bluebells

It is April in England, and the rolling hills and forests are starting to bud and bristle with bright green signs of life. But on the forest floor, a different color runs wild and takes hold.

The winter is gone, washed away by billowing spring showers. Change is coming, and magic hangs in the air as the ancient woodlands start to awaken.

In the sun-dappled forest dells of the south coast, where the air is the warmest in the UK, something magical is springing from the thawing brown earth.

The forest floor, once brown and dull, is slowly moving as a powerful force pushes up and out. Green shoots spring up around the bases of trees, stumps, burrows, piles of leaves, and everything in between.

In almost no time, the little stems grow grapelike blobs, which blossom into tiny, perfect little rows of bells, such as a fairy might wear as a springtime bonnet. The rolling miniature world of magnificent bells shakes in the springtime breeze.

This fairytale blanket of blue creeps up the length of the country from bottom to top in just a few magical weeks, and then disappears as fast as it crept! The flowers carry a message of spring tidings across the oldest, wildest, and most forgotten parts of this isle, paving the way for summer.

NORWAY
A Drop of Rain

The ice is melting on the tops of the mountains that surround Geirangerfjord. A little water droplet springs from the warming glacier and rolls down the greening mountainside. Plop! It falls into the calm waters below. But this is just the start of its journey, as April showers wake up the fjord from its winter sleep and this little drop of water becomes part of an endless cycle.

The warmer spring air is thawing out the majestic mountains, but the water in the fjord is still icy cold from winter.

When the little droplet drips into the ice-blue fjord, the warm air above starts to turn the tip-top layer of water into misty air.

The little drop is floating in the sky now; up and up the warm air pushes the mist, and it forms into a cloud.

The cloud grows darker and fuller. As more drops join it, the cloud becomes too heavy to hold them all in.

As the cloud is blown onto the mountain edge, the drop falls, along with millions of others, and begins its journey back down the mountainside.

As they cascade, some drops are drunk by the thirsty plants that grow ever greener on the mountain.

But this drop plops back into the cold fjord below. Joining the millions of other drops that form the shimmering lake, it swirls and waits for its next trip into the clouds, ready to wash the winter off the spring mountains, and water them for summer.

JAPAN
A Snow Dance

It is April in the north of Japan, and the ground is blanketed in magical, pure white snow. In the bright sun, icy crystals glitter and the scene is set for something special. It is the perfect stage for a spectacularly romantic dance.

Among the many cranes in the flock, two young birds spot each other. They lock eyes, beginning to move towards one another and into an icy clearing.

The principal dancers in this evening's performance are the most famous and rare of creatures: red-crowned cranes. Their magnificent, circular red caps look just like the red center of the Japanese flag. It is only natural that they have become a symbol of Japan.

The stage is set, blanketed in snow. Starting far away from each other, they throw back their heads and let out an earth-shattering honk in perfect, noisy unison. It is not a beautiful song, but to a crane, the honking sound from their dance partner is sweet music.

Then they begin to dance. Like two ballerinas in a *pas de deux*, or dance duet, they weave around each other—coming closer, then hopping away, in rhythmic formations and dramatic twists and turns. They move in perfect harmony.

The more they dance, the more these lovebirds are bound closer together. Now they will be dance partners for life, coming back to this spot every year to spend long evenings dancing, and eventually raising a chick together.

This dance will bond them for a long life together, which is why in Japan these birds are symbols of loyalty and longevity. In myth, they are said to live for 1,000 years. In reality they live for around 50 years, but the beauty of their regular dance is as timeless and enduring as the changing of the seasons.

SAUDI ARABIA
A Dust Storm in the Desert

The Rub' al-Khali is one of the hottest and driest places in the world. The heat hums in the still air, making mirages across the sand. But as the heat begins to climb at the beginning of May, winds start to whip up almighty storms.

Saudi Arabia is 95 percent desert, and the earth is always hot and dry. The bright blue sky above and the hot orange sand below are perfect, bright opposites.

But as the summer winds start to sweep in across the desert in fast, warm breaths, sand is thrown up to 50 feet into the air! These fluffy, billowing clouds of dust tear across the land, turning the sky as orange as the desert below. The air and the ground become one.

As the Sun dips below the horizon, the land cools a little and the clouds of dust settle. But this is just the first of many summer sandstorms, which can turn bright, blistering day into swirling, cloudy night in a single hot puff of air.

USA
A Magical Moonbow

On a sunny spring day with moments of rain, you might be lucky enough to see a rainbow stretch across the sky. Light shines through the droplets of water and fractures into bands of different colors. But at this time of year, under a large spring Moon in Yosemite National Park, as if by some stroke of fairy magic, a moonbow appears.

It is a cloudless night in Yosemite National Park, and the stars shine bright in the pitch-black sky.

But the night is far from still.
Nighttime animals wake up and begin to prowl.
Their way is lit by a huge, full spring Moon shining down between the trees. The great horned owl takes wing from her perch and swoops over the bottom of the great falls that crash into the pool.

The Moon is at its brightest and closest to Earth, and it drenches the great falls in eerie light. Moonlight is not made by the Moon. It is a reflection of the Sun's light, bouncing off our Moon's milky surface.

The cold, blueish moonlight passes through the tiny droplets of waterfall mist and is split into all of the different colors of light.

The mist made by the crashing water rises up into the air above the pool and, suddenly, something magical starts to shimmer into view.

Moonbows are some of the rarest of nature's treasures, because they need lots of things to be just right. The night must be clear. And most importantly, it must be the exact moment in the Moon's cycle when it is brightest and closest to Earth, so that the light is strong enough for its beams to be filtered by the mist.

SOUTH AFRICA

The Great Sardine Run

SOUTH
AFRICA

Agulhas
Bank

It is May in South Africa, which spells the end of the hot summer. As the air cools, so does the glistening sea around the southernmost tip of the craggy, wild coast. As soon as the water drops below 70°F at the Agulhas Bank, billions of sardines start to have their babies.

The sea glistens with the bright scales of energetic little fish with only one thing on their minds—following the current of cool seawater moving up the east coast.

This is one of the biggest underwater migrations on the planet, and billions of little fish moving as one cause quite a splash. Hungry creatures from far and wide start to gather, waiting for the traveling feast to pass through.

First, the Cape fur seals take their chances, but this shoal is so big that they find it hard to isolate any fish to eat. Even though the fish are small, they have power in numbers.

Next, fierce tuna attack from below and push the twinkling clouds closer to the dangerous surface.

Now that the sardines are near the surface, shearwater birds dive down onto them from the air. They are excellent fliers and agile underwater, but they can only snap up one fish at a time.

Sensing the blood in the water, next to arrive are the copper sharks. They tumble and crash into the ever-tighter shoals, coming out with mouths full of teeth and scales. The predators never attack one another. Instead, they take turns to grab a mouthful of fish.

The waters are white with the feeding frenzy!

When the drama is nearly over, last of all comes a Bryde's whale to finish off the feast. After the chaotic action, this giant glides through the water, scooping up hundreds of fish at once.

The lucky sardines who make it up the gauntlet of the east coast are rewarded with a peaceful winter. They have lived to tell the tale of the great sardine run!

TRINIDAD
The Flying Guava Farmer

This little leaf-nosed bat has a very important job, and she takes it seriously. May is a busy time in her line of work—and to do the job well, she needs to be very thirsty.

It is spring in Trinidad, and the flowers in the forest where this leaf-nosed bat lives are bursting into bloom. But even a Trinidad spring day is much too hot for a furry bat, and so she spends it sleeping in the shade of a big banana leaf.

The Sun has set, and she has woken up with an empty tummy and a big job to do. She flies all over the forest in search of flowers. At nighttime, the flowers that get her attention aren't the colorful ones that attract bees during the day, but milky-white ones that stand out in the darkness.

She flits towards a branch filled with bright white, frilly guava flowers and slicks her long tongue into the middle of a bloom. She drinks the delicious nectar inside—and as she does so, she gets a little dusting of pollen on her fur.

When she flies over to the next guava tree, some of the pollen from the first tree rubs off onto the next tree's flowers.

In this way she spreads pollen to hundreds of guava flowers in the forest, from tree to tree. This is called pollination, and the guava flowers need it to happen before they can turn into fruit.

Now that the flowers are pollinated, the fruit can start to grow. Our little bat is like a guava farmer, making sure that the plants have what they need in order to grow their fruit.

The reward for her hard work will come in August, when the fruit is ripe and she can eat as many pieces as she likes!

USA

A Light Show in the Forest

It is a hot night in June, and night has fallen on the tall trees of the Great Smoky Mountains. As the last light disappears from the sky, something magical is happening.

It looks as though a galaxy of twinkling stars has come to rest among the trees. But these are thousands of fireflies, or lightning bugs, flashing the tips of their tails to try to attract a mate.

During this one special week, male fireflies flash their tails on and off 5–8 times, pause for 8 seconds, and then repeat the pattern. Interested females light up their tails in reply.

This twinkling, synchronized display is one of the most magical shows on Earth.

INDONESIA
A Spectacular Stink

It is the middle of June, and the high tropical rainforests of Sumatra are humming with life. The air is perfumed by humid soil and sweet pollen from flowers competing for the bugs' attention. But the show is about to be stolen by the stinkiest of spectacles.

In a small clearing, a huge green spike has been growing from the orange soil at enormous speed.

With no leaves around it, this green trunk is bulging in the middle and growing fatter by the day.

One afternoon, as the sun hits the tip of its spike, the green torpedo begins to unfurl. It slowly opens, becoming a single, enormous bloom.

This bloom is one of the most attention-seeking in the world, lasting only for 48 hours. In this time, it needs to steal the show from every other flower in the forest. It does this by being smelly—very smelly. Bugs are attracted from far and wide by its special stench of rotting flesh!

The bloom stays open all night long, and captures the attention of thousands of bugs. They bring it pollen from the blooms they have visited before. This is what it needs to make seeds.

After the long, putrid-smelling night, the bloom has what it needs and it starts to wither away, channeling its energy into growing seeds. Eventually, the whole process will begin again.

ENGLAND
A Total Eclipse of the Moon

June is the middle of the eclipse season in the northern hemisphere.
It is a time of year when, in the dead of one or two nights, the Moon
almost disappears. But what does it mean, and where does it go?

The very end of Lizard Point in Cornwall is the most southerly tip
of the British mainland. The wide-open sea stretches
for miles beyond this craggy cove.

High above the sea shines the
Moon, pulling in the tides and waves day and
night. But tonight, for a brief spell, the Moon
appears to take a break.

Even on ordinary nights, clouds float in front of the Moon sometimes. But tonight it disappears almost completely.

The Moon's glow is secondhand; it reflects light from the Sun back to Earth. But tonight, the Earth has moved right in front of the Sun, so the Moon is in the Earth's shadow.

The Moon turns a dark, spooky red color for nearly two hours, and the lapping waters coming into shore look pitch black.

But after its rest the Moon returns just as before, and shines down on the sparkling sea.

PALESTINE
A Stay at the Fig Hotel

It is June, and this huge fig tree is growing lots of little fruits along its dry branches. First, they appear as tiny hard green bulbs. But the fruits have to ripen, and the tree can't make them do so on its own. It needs the helping hand of its most important guest of the year, and June is open season at the fig hotel.

A little wasp is ready to lay her eggs, but she needs a safe place to keep them while they grow. She knows just the place.

She flies to a little green fig bulb and begins to burrow into the skin at the bottom of the fruit. As she crawls through a narrow tunnel to the middle, pollen from the fig bulb that she was born in rubs onto the fruit. This pollen is the missing ingredient that the fig needs to ripen.

Once the eggs hatch, the males dig tunnels out of the fruit. This helps the females to fly away and start their own new lives and families.

These two living things are very different, and yet they rely on each other to survive. The fig needs the wasp to stay, and the wasp needs the safety of her room at the fig hotel.

In return for giving the fruit the pollen it needs, the fig provides a safe, private room for the wasp to lay her eggs.

FRANCE
The Winds of Change

It is July in the hot southern French countryside. Cicadas chirrup in humming lavender rows and fruit hangs still and sweet on the trees. The only movement is the heads of thousands of sunflowers, turning to follow the Sun across the sky.

But the mistral is coming—a shock of cool air from the north that wreaks havoc on the summer stillness.

Its name means "masterful," and it changes the mood of everything around. Some say it even changes people's personalities while it blows.

In reality, the wind is caused by the summer temperatures creating a build-up of pressure. But it feels like Mother Nature reminding us that even in the stale air of blissful calm and fruitfulness, change can arrive out of nowhere.

KENYA
The Great Migration

Every year, millions of wildebeest make a treacherous and dramatic journey to the grasslands in Kenya. They face danger along the way, but there is a sweet reward waiting for them.

This wildebeest is one in a million. She is mighty, powerful, and ever so huge.

But she is small in a herd so big that it can be seen from space. The herd contains friends and family, strangers, and familiar faces. From the day she was born to the end of her life, she will spend every single day on the move.

But where is she going, across the big, dry Serengeti? What are they all searching for? And who is leading the way? They are looking for water to drink, but there's not much of it about. Thankfully, tracking the rain clouds comes as naturally to wildebeest as falling asleep.

Rain has fallen over 30 miles away. Without quite knowing how, the whole herd can sense it, and they all begin to move as one.

They run over rolling plains, gathering pace and heading towards the Mara River. They reach the steep edge, but there is no way to stop the charging herd! Over the edge of the riverbank they tumble. Splash!

Our wildebeest is hard to spot among the wild water and swirling animals. Some wildebeest dart off down the river, avoiding a hungry lion. Others swerve the hungry crocodiles who snap at their heels.

River-drenched and exhausted, she is safely carried along in the mass of the crowd—into the plains of Kenya. Eventually, they reach the site where the rains have fallen. It now swishes with tasty grasses.

USA
Life from the Ashes

Fire is frightening to almost all living things, but there is an exception to every rule. Forests are often tinder-dry in Oregon in the month of July, the heady smell of sap sitting hot and heavy in the air. One tree patiently waits for a spark. It has made something special that can only be unlocked by a flame.

A year ago, a lodgepole tree dropped its cone, but the seeds within are locked inside a hard outer coating that is glued shut with resin.

The rain came and nothing happened. The cone didn't grow like the other seeds in the forest did.

But in the middle of the night in hot July, the dry forest bursts into flame! The flames tear though the forest, shriveling up the leaves of plants and sending animals running for their lives.

But our pine cone is warming. The pressure inside it builds up until it bursts!

Now that the seed is free, it is ready to grow—just as soon as the fire passes and the cool rain falls.

Out of the scorched earth comes new life. The tree that will grow from this pine cone is a reminder that even the most terrible things can plant the seed of something good.

ITALY
The Wood Wide Web

In the ancient Vallombrosa Forest in Italy, a little sapling sprang up at the start of the year. Now it is growing taller and forming more tough bark around its middle. But the hot summer is here now, and try as it might, its little roots can't find enough water to drink. It is much smaller than the other trees, and it isn't getting any of the summer sunshine that it needs to live. In the dark heat of July, this little tree must ask the forest for help. But how?

Every tree, even the smallest, has roots. They grow down far underground; some trees' root systems are as deep underground as their branches are tall above the ground.

So far, this little tree has only used her roots to soak up water and goodness from the soil. But she has run out of what she needs, and every fiber of her being is sending a message of distress. Who will listen? She feels very small and very alone.

Luckily, her little roots are also connected to tiny underground fibers of fungus. Each strand of fungus may be small, but it is part of a web that sits under the entire forest floor and connects every single living plant beneath the soil.

These webs of fungus are like a super-fast broadband connection between every single tree in the whole forest.

"HELP! LITTLE TREE NEEDS WATER AND ENERGY!"

"I AM SICK, AND I DON'T HAVE THE ENERGY TO SPARE," says one tree.

"I AM STILL GROWING, AND I HARDLY HAVE ENOUGH LIGHT FOR MYSELF," says another.

As the fungus picks up on the distress signals from the tiny tree, it sends out the message to all the big, tall trees nearby.

But the Mother Tree, the oldest and largest of them all replies, "I AM HUNDREDS OF YEARS OLD, AND I HAVE PLENTY OF SPARE SUGARS AND WATER IN MY TRUNK."

And so the big, tall Mother Tree sends sugars along the fungus pathways, all the way to the little tree in need.

This little tree isn't alone after all. She is part of what is called the "Wood Wide Web." This network connects her to a community of others, who have supported each other for many hundreds of years.

In the future, when the little tree is taller and stronger, she, too, will help others in need. She may even warn them of any dangers, such as pesky fruit-nibbling aphids or tree diseases doing the rounds.

Every tree is part of a living, breathing family which look after each other. Just like a family, the strength of the forest comes from being able to ask for and to give help. A forest is only as healthy as it's littlest tree.

August

TASMANIA
The Aurora Australis

Many things that happen on Earth have an opposite. The northern lights have an opposite that lives in the skies of Tasmania. In the month of August, an eerie light begins to dance across the sky. This is the aurora australis, or the southern lights. It is the sister of the aurora borealis, the northern lights.

The South Pole has as strong a magnetic force as the North Pole, and it attracts charged particles that dance in the air as light.

Like an identical twin, the aurora australis looks similar to its northern sister, but has its own personality. Instead of reflecting off ice floes, this aurora dances on warm waters by sandy Australian shores.

SRI LANKA
A Gathering of Giants

It has been another long, hot dry season in Sri Lanka. Many animals are struggling to find enough water to drink, and there is still a month or so to go until the rainy season arrives. But the most important event in the elephants' year is about to take place.

They reach a dark forest, but there is no time to dawdle. Mum pats her brave baby on the trunk and tells her that they must not fall behind: there is a very important appointment that they cannot miss.

This baby elephant is not quite a year old, but her family is taking her on a very long walk. All the family, big and small, walk for days. They are dreaming of cool water, but the rainy monsoon season is still many weeks away.

When they emerge from the trees, they see
the orange sun setting over a huge plain.
In the middle is a big, shimmering lake.
It's like something from a dream.

Just as baby begins to take her first sip of cool
water, she notices hundreds of shadowy giants
striding out from the trees around the plain.

Soon the water is asplash with elephants who
look just like her! It is the biggest meeting of
Asian elephants anywhere on the planet.

Every year for the rest of her life she will come
back to this annual meeting of the giants. And each
time, it will be the most refreshing—
and sociable—sip of water of the year.

No one is quite sure how these elephants remember
when to come back, but one thing is certain: an
elephant never forgets.

MALDIVES
A Sea of Glowing Stars

Even after night has fallen and everyone has gone to bed, the ever-rolling waves never take a rest. On most beaches around the world, the tumbling seawater is dark as night. But in some special places, the waves wash in millions of what seem like tiny glowing stars.

Dusk falls on Vaadhoo island in the Maldives. It is the end of a long, long day of sunshine, twinkling on clear blue waters and sparkling on hot white sand.

As the air begins to cool and the calming wash rolls in, the tiny waves are churning up something magical.

The neon glow is actually millions of microscopic plankton in the water, causing a special spectacle called bioluminescence. These plankton have evolved over millions of years to surprise anything that disturbs them by suddenly letting out bright light, as if to say, "Leave us alone!" When the waves crash, the plankton are startled and let out their luminescent glow.

The result is a shore that glows with a billion tiny glittering stars, like an underwater night sky.

CHINA
A Bamboo Bear House

It is late August in Sichuan, and a female panda suddenly has something very important to get ready for.

This female giant panda's daily life is not usually that busy. She really doesn't have much on, and she's been feeling particularly tired recently! She wakes up, stretches, scratches, and goes about her day... slowly.

She doesn't have many natural predators, so she never has to run anywhere fast.

She doesn't even have to travel for food; she lives in a lush forest full of her favorite (and only) snack: bamboo.

But something is about to change—and she must get organized, quicky! She collects a large pile of bamboo and soft leaves, and starts to make it into a cosy nest.

The nest is ready just in time, because the very next morning, she gives birth to a tiny baby panda cub.

He is born with his eyes shut and almost no fur. Over the next few months he will grow a fuzzy black-and-white coat and open his eyes. But for now, he is safe and sound in his bamboo bear house.

September

SPAIN
A Mushroom Grows in a Forest

Once the weather starts to cool in the Basque Country and there is a chill around the trees, magical white mushrooms start to push their pale caps through the damp earth.

The wet fall has watered a fungus that starts to grow. It starts life as a little spore: a tiny seed too small to see with your eyes.

As it starts to grow, it sends out little roots below the soil. When it bumps into roots from another spore, it begins to form a mushroom, or "fruiting body." At first, this looks like a little ball.

Unlike plants, this porcini mushroom doesn't need light to grow. Instead, it pushes up and out into the moist, dark air of the shady forest.

In September, the damp forest floor is turned into a fairytale scene of toadstools and mushrooms. Some are very poisonous, and some have spots on that say, "Stay away!"

When the time comes, the porcini mushroom releases a cloud of spores. They are carried on the air and then land, ready to grow next fall.

CANADA
A Salmon's Quest

After a long life growing strong in the wide open seas, a big, powerful salmon turns fin and begins her last adventure. It will be a lengthy and dangerous swim to the top of the river where, once upon a time, she was born.

She reaches the river mouth and uses her muscular body to swim against the current.

She flings her body up, up, up the rushing waterfalls. But they are not all that stand in her way: hungry bears sit by the rapids, waiting for her to catapult herself out of the protection of the water.

Some of her friends become a fish supper for the grizzly family, but our plucky salmon keeps on. Day and night she swims: to rest, even for a moment, would mean washing back down the river.

After many days and almost 900 miles of exhausting swimming and aerial acrobatics, she has reached the end of her quest. And she has carried something special all the way here. A sac in the underside of her body is filled with tiny eggs, which she releases into the water.

Each egg clings to a pebble near the gentle edge of the calm pools.

Our brave salmon's life's work is now complete. But her strength will live on in her little babies, once they hatch and swim back down the river to start their lives in the ocean.

INDIA
The Home of the Clouds

Meghalaya means "the home of the clouds" in the Sanskrit language, but this magical place is right here on Earth, in India. September is the last month of the monsoon season, when this place comes alive. At this time of year, the heavens empty onto the hot land. Life and lush green forests are washed and watered by the heaviest rains anywhere on Earth.

Close to the clouds, this is the home of rain—and September is one of the rainiest months of the year. Rain here falls in big splashing drops and is carried across the tops of trees on gusts of strong wind. It transforms the whole landscape.

Elephant Falls has burst into life, carrying huge white cascades of water over the top of the valley's edge and down into its folds.

The whole valley floor turns a rich emerald green, as plant life springs up as far as the eye can see.

The monsoon season turns the forest landscape into a colorful world, fed and painted by water—reminding us that it is the most precious element.

JAMAICA
The Hermit Crabs' House Swap

A baby hermit crab has been swimming throughout its wilderness months, without a home or responsibilities to weigh him down. Now, maturity is coming—and so, too, must home ownership. But how to get onto the property ladder, and how to find the right shell?

This little crab was born in the spring and has been growing up fast, dining on abundant plankton in the warm Caribbean seas. Now, at the end of the long Jamaican summer, he puts claw to sand for the first time since hatching.

Looking for the perfect home, he stumbles upon a large, echoing conch shell. He scampers all over it. It is far too big for him. But there are no other homes around! Whatever will he do?

A mid-sized hermit crab scuttles up the beach towards him, looking to try his luck with the palatial shell. He is outgrowing his own shell, but this new home is still too roomy even for him.

Soon, lots of other crabs have gathered from around the
shoreline. Everyone is looking for an upgrade after growing
a little bigger over the summer.

The group of crabs size each other up. Now that
they have the measure of things, they organize
themselves in an orderly queue from biggest to
smallest. But none of them is big enough for the
conch shell.

Finally, a huge, wise old hermit arrives. Her
shell is getting a little tight, and this new find is
UST right. She leaves her shell and moves into
the giant conch. In turn, everyone else moves
up a shell size, too.

After all the crabs have moved in, a perfectly sized tiny first home is left for
our little crab. Every few months, as he grows, he will make his way further
along the queue. Maybe one day he will be big and wise enough to fill
a giant conch of his own.

October

USA
A Falling Leaf

In the leaf-dense forests of New England, crowds of trees and their millions of leaves are about to part from each other.

It has been a luscious long summer for this little leaf. But it started as just a bright green bud.

Then it grew into its full, noble green span. It has rustled in the warm summer breeze, tickled by the others on its branch.

It has been washed many times by flashes of summer rain, and glistened in the night under crashes of hot summer lightning.

But now winter is coming: a season that it knows isn't for little leaves. And so, it must fall to the ground soon.

As the leaves give out, they burn brighter than ever before. Like the last flickers of heat before the cold winter, the trees appear to burst into bright flames of red and orange, in celebration of the year they have had together. The whole landscape is alive with life-force orange. Finally, the winter darkness descends, not to be pierced again until the next green buds arrive in spring.

WESTERN NEW GUINEA
The Perfect Nest

This is the story of the plainest—but proudest—little bird in the whole forest. For the male Vogelkop bowerbird, October means showtime. But will his eye for design and the finer things on the forest floor win him love?

These little birds may have drab brown feathers, but they have a very appreciative eye for color. This one has unique taste: he prefers orange and blue things. He has scoured the forest for fruit and flowers that fit best with his color scheme.

Once he has found them, he puts them in place outside his tidy bower: a tiny hut that he has woven from sticks. He even lays a luxurious carpet of moss, fit for a king—or more precisely, a queen.

But not everything he finds for the display plays ball. This Ulysses butterfly is the right color, but doesn't stick around to become part of the collection.

He wants to find love. But competition is tough: other birds have beautiful bowers, too, filled with differently colored petals and trinkets.

The day of judgment is here! A female Vogelkop bowerbird arrives. She looks around all of the bowers before selecting her favorite. She chooses the most impressive nest, with the most impressive singer inside.

Luckily for this little bird, she simply cannot resist blue.

VENEZUELA
A Lightning Spectacular

It is the peak of the rainy season, and Mother Nature is preparing to put on a spectacular show. One of the longest-running daily performances in the natural calendar, it happens on up to 300 days of the year, with each show lasting up to 9 hours. The stage is always the same: Lake Maracaibo in Venezuela. Expect dramatic flashes in the most bombastic show on Earth!

Lake Maracaibo is a large bay on the edge of the Caribbean Sea. It is filled by both the sea and the Catatumbo river, which flows into it. Over the dry season the river was low, and the air was warm and still.

The natural shape of the lake forces wind to blow in from the sea and up the sides of the mountains all around.

But when the rain comes, water flows and swirls into the lake—and it is not just the water that is churned up.

Half a mile above the river-mouth, the air becomes charged with electricity, which is then released in hot flashes of lightning. They crack over the lake around 28 times per minute.

The show has been a near-nightly performance for many thousands of years. Even a nighttime attack on the city of Maracaibo, led by Sir Francis Drake in 1595, was exposed by the flashes of light from the raging bolts of lightning.

To add to the air of mystery, the lightning is so high up in the sky that the show is as silent as an old film!

RUSSIA
Brown Bear's Bedtime

In Siberia, the summer has been mild. But now that fall is waning and winter is on the horizon, it is time for brown bears to get ready for bed.

This bear is getting ready for bed— but she isn't brushing her teeth or having a bath. Getting ready takes her several weeks, and there is a lot to do. This bedtime is no ordinary one: she is going to sleep right through from October until May! This long winter sleep is called hibernation.

First, she needs to eat a whole winter's worth of food. During October she can eat up to 90 pounds per day of nuts, berries, small furry animals, fish, and whatever else she can get her claws on. She can walk for hundreds of miles to find all the food she needs. When she sleeps, she will survive on the fat she stores from these huge meals.

Next, she needs to find the perfect spot. She scours the landscape and finds herself a little cave in a hillside, hollowed out by some tree roots. This will be the perfect cosy shelter to keep her safe below the ground, away from icy winds, until spring.

Now that she is ready for bed, she climbs into her underground nest. She has prepared her body well—but when she wakes up, her life will have changed.

She has made sure that she has extra fat reserves this year, because hibernation is going to be a little different. She is pregnant! When spring comes, she will not emerge from her snug cave alone. There will be two small bear cubs by her side, tumbling out into the Siberian spring.

November

ALGERIA
Snow in the Desert

A little fennec fox lives deep in the Sahara Desert in Algeria. So far, she has only known hot weather. But during an unusual cold snap in November, something unexpected is about to happen.

The Sahara Desert is one of the driest places on Earth, as well as one of the hottest. This little fennec is perfectly adapted to deal with the heat: her big ears help her to radiate out any extra warmth.

But this year, the world's changing climate and unpredictable winters are about to cause something incredible to happen. Something that this fennec and her radiating ears were not quite expecting.

A little flake of snow falls on her giant ears. What an unusual feeling! By the next morning, a dusting of snow has zebra-striped its way over the undulating sand dunes.

As the climate changes, so does our landscape—and this little fennec fox has never felt so thankful to have a thick, furry coat.

1.

The mother albatross preens her feathers and leaves the place that has been her home for a year. She spreads her huge wings; they are almost 11 feet across. She looks enormous and regal, taking flight in the sky above the Southern Ocean.

2.

Sailors and famous writers have admired her for hundreds of years. One called her a "regal, feathery thing of unspotted whiteness."

ANTARCTICA
The Longest Flight

7.

When she returns, she meets her trusty mate— the father of all of her children. After a year of adventuring apart, they affectionately greet, and get ready to start another little family.

6.

This is her life for a whole year: eating, flying, and sleeping.

3.

She flies fast without flapping her wings, using a clever technique called "dynamic soaring": she locks her gigantic wings in place for several hours at a time, and glides up and down currents in the wind. She can fly at up to three times the speed of the wind, traveling 620 miles per day.

A pair of wandering albatross parents are coming to the end of a long year, spent raising a chick together on Prince Edward Island off the coast of South Africa. Raising a baby here is tough, but they have done well. Their little one hatched in April, and now by November it has flown the nest. Its mum and dad are getting ready for a well-deserved wilderness year doing what they do best: wandering.

5.

She keeps the South Pole on one side of her the whole time, and this way she will eventually circle Antarctica. Some years she may even circle it up to three times, taking in the best fish and squid along the way, before coming back to the same spot that she first left.

4.

But where is she going so fast? She is flying quite literally around the world, in search of her favorite things to eat. She dives and swallows a juicy squid. Sleeping off a big dinner is no problem, even when she is far out at sea. Our clever albatross catches forty winks en route.

ZAMBIA
Life Comes Flooding Back

In November, the Zambian side of the Victoria Falls is a dry precipice. Months of hot sun and no rain have left it craggy and bare, but the year is about to turn on a dime as life comes rushing back.

Dust blows down the dry, craggy cliff that separates Zambia from its neighbor, Zimbabwe. It has been months since the earth here felt water running over its edges.

But today, as if from nowhere, a little trickle of water makes its way through the dust and begins to drip over the side of the crevasse.

Further up the parched riverbed, the rain has arrived. It falls slowly at first. Then it falls quickly and hard.

It fills the riverbed—every drop seems to be in a race to reach the side of the falls and cascade down into the pool below.

The water brings drama back to the landscape. The waterfalls flow once more, delivering much-needed water to plants and animals all over the land.

POLAND
A New Coat for Winter

This little brown mountain hare is eight months old. She was born in March, and she grew up while the sun was shining and the whole of Białowieża Forest was warm and abuzz with life. She spent the summer getting stronger, learning how to forage and find the tastiest lichens and lush leaves to eat. But with winter comes a magical surprise.

There isn't anything about this forest that this little hare doesn't know. She wears a clever coat of brown fur, which camouflages her perfectly against the forest floor. Even if an enemy spots her, she can run to safety quick as a flash! This little hare knows how to look after herself, no problem—easy.

Until… something strange happens. A tiny white snowflake drops onto her twitchy brown nose, and a chilly wind whips through the forest.

At the same time, she spots that one of her little hairs is silvery white. This is very strange. Every one of her other hairs is brown.

The wind has blown ever colder overnight and brought with it a dusting of snow. Almost all the hairs on her little face have turned white.

Each day brings
a thicker blanket of
snow, and more
white hairs.

The little hare and the
forest both turn an icy white
together, from the snow-
laden branches to her fluffy
white tail.

Feeling splendid, the
proud hare bounds
through the snow. Only
her black-tipped ears
are showing.

Dressed by Mother Nature in her winter
best, the little hare is hidden from any
enemies as she leaps through the drifts.

December

PORTUGAL
A Night Owl Hunts by Day

In the depths of winter, the cold Sun comes up over a bare vineyard in Portugal. A snowy white-bellied barn owl, who usually only hunts at night, glides on silent wings between the rows of vines, looking for life.

Generally, this barn owl hunts by night. Her feather-soft wingbeats and the cover of darkness help her to sneak up on field mice and make a meal of them.

But in midwinter, her favorite furry snacks are mostly hiding beneath the ground, holed up with stores of food carefully stowed away during the warmer months.

This makes life hard for the owl, who can only pick off the disorganized or daring mice and voles who venture out into the exposed field.

Less food means longer hunting hours. Although the winter nights are at their longest, this owl's hunting day is longer still. She must fly over the hard earth even in the cold light of day.

NAMIBIA
A Desert Drink

Mid-December is the hot season in the Namib Desert, and life is dry and tough. This is one of the driest places on Earth, and only the hardiest creatures can survive here. But one clever little beetle has found a way of conjuring up the key ingredient for staying alive—from thin air.

In the early morning quiet, a little beetle stirs from her nest under the sand. She has a special, almost magical task on her mind, and it is best done in the cool of the small hours.

Even though the magnificent Namib Desert stretches along the seashore, there is not a drop of water to be found in the ground. For the creatures and plants who live here, it is almost impossible to find a life-giving drink.

The little beetle sets off from home and heads up, up, up the tallest sand dune she can find. She walks up the side of the dune that faces out towards the sea.

After a tiring walk past tumbling grains of sand, she decides that she is high enough. She points her head down and sticks her bottom up to the sky! Her wings are now pointing upwards, but instead of taking flight, she simply waits.

As the Sun comes up, the heat makes fog rise from the sea and billow in over the soon-to-be sun-drenched desert.

When the fog arrives, our little beetle is ready. As the fog hits her wings, tiny droplets of water from the air are channeled between bumps on her body, and they flow down into her open mouth. "Drrrrrip!"

With the help of her rough, outstretched body, she has trapped herself a delicious and much-needed drink.

NORWAY
The Sky Ablaze

In the deep, dark winter's night, there are few places colder than the icy Arctic plains of Norway. The sky is so dark and empty, and the nights are so long, that it feels as though only a miracle could break their endlessness. But tonight, something miraculous is about to happen.

A paintbrush-sweep of eerie green breaks across the night sky. The color moves and flows, like a drop of ink spreading through water. Purples and pinks bleed into the moving work of art in the sky.

The snowy landscape below gleams with the strange light cast by the northern lights, or the aurora borealis.

These amazing light shows are not the work of invading aliens. They are caused by winds, carrying special charged particles that have blown all the way from the Sun.

All through the long Norwegian winter, the dark, cold nights are brightened by these reminders of color and energy, while the frozen land sleeps in ice below

SCOTLAND
A Highland Feast

In the ancient Caledonian Forest in the Scottish Highlands, the earth is hard and blanketed in heavy snow. The winter solstice, the shortest day of the year, signals the very middle of winter. But things are far from bleak for a certain russet-colored, twitchy-whiskered resident, for whom the whole frozen forest is a well-stocked pantry.

Hopping into a clearing is a bright-eyed red squirrel. A few months ago, she set about burying nuts all over the forest floor. She buried a particularly tasty one near a notable-looking tree stump.

Now all she has to do is remember where it is.

This one isn't right.

This one might have been right, but someone else seems to have got here first.

Finally, she finds the right one. That tree stump does look familiar!

At the base of the tree is a big, delicious nut.

This is just one of the many sweet, nutty snacks that will keep this clever creature warm and fed until spring comes and the forest begins to bloom with tasty treats again.

INDEX

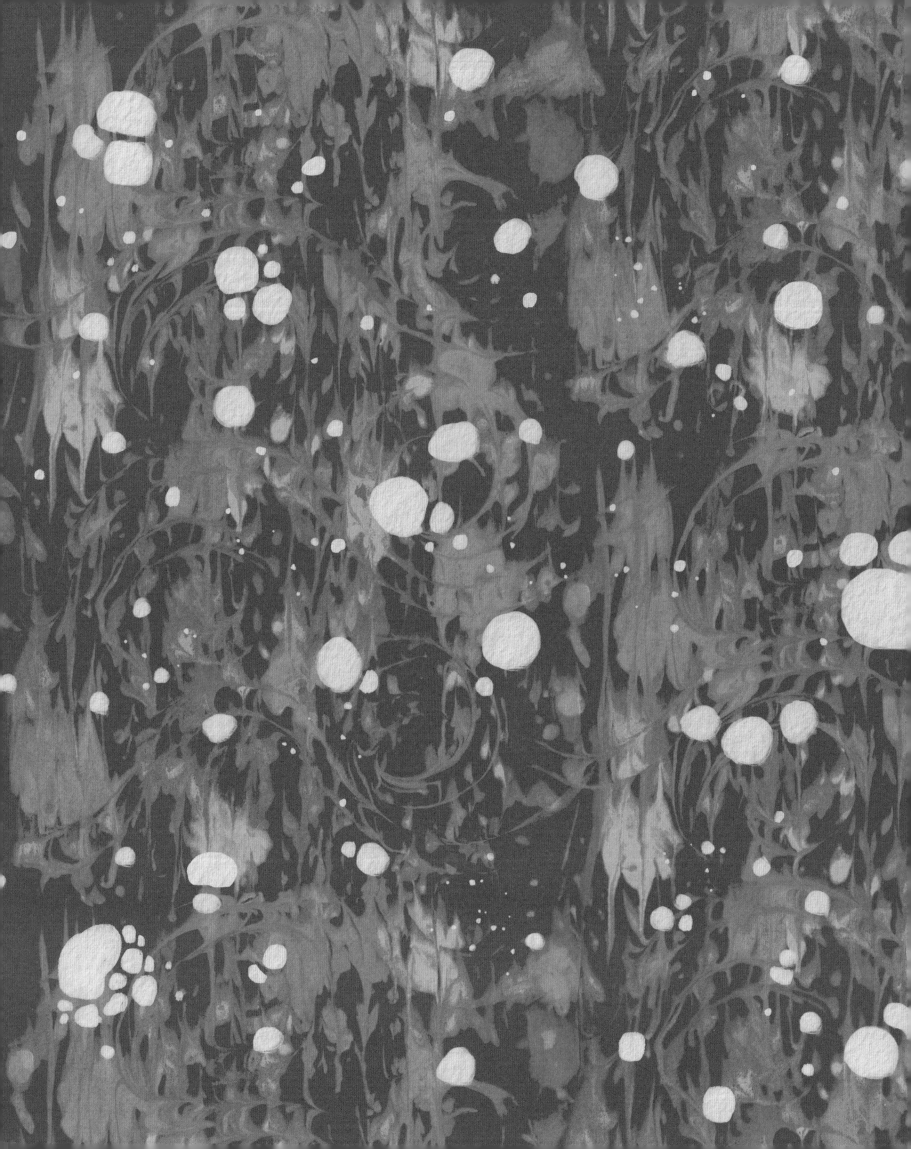

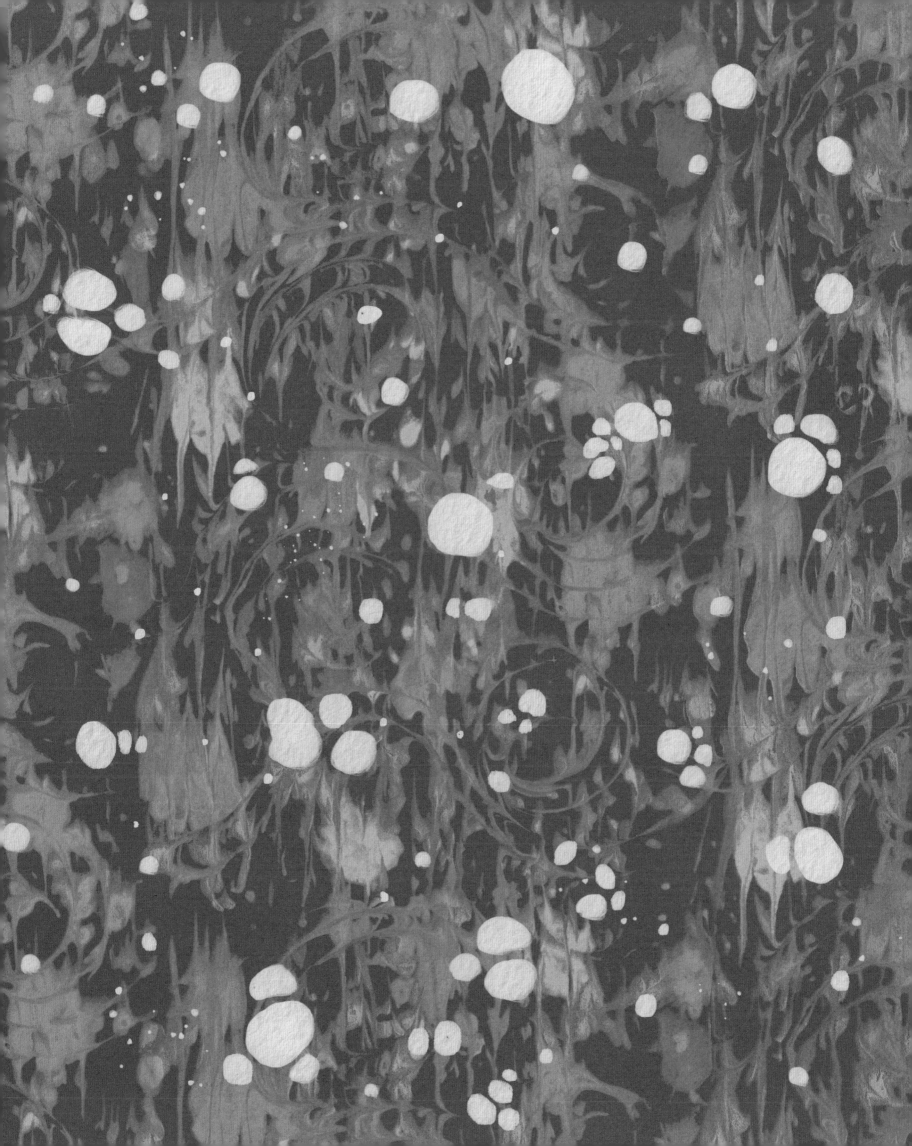